DANIEL BOONE
AND THE
AMERICAN WEST

Robin May

Illustrated by Gerry Wood

LIFE AND TIMES

Julius Caesar and the Romans
Alfred the Great and the Saxons
Canute and the Vikings
William the Conqueror and the Normans
Richard the Lionheart and the Crusades
Columbus and the Age of Exploration
Montezuma and the Aztecs
Elizabeth I and Tudor England
Oliver Cromwell and the Civil War
Daniel Boone and the American West

Further titles are in preparation.

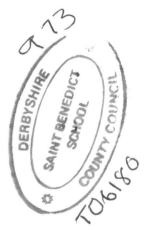
First published in 1985 by
Wayland (Publishers) Ltd
49, Lansdowne Place, Hove
East Sussex BN3 1HF, England

© Copyright 1985 Wayland (Publishers) Ltd

ISBN 0 85078 556 1

Phototypeset by Planagraphic Typesetters Ltd
Printed in Italy by G. Canale & C.S.p.A., Turin
Bound in the U.K. by The Pitman Press, Bath

Contents

1 THE STORY OF DANIEL BOONE
Young explorer 4
Hunter and soldier 6
The legend 8

2 THE FIRST AMERICANS
Discovery and settlement 10
From colony to superpower 12

3 MOVING WESTWARDS
Land hunger 14
Covered wagons 16
Gold rush! 18
Steamboats and stages 20
Rails across the West 22

4 NATIVE AMERICANS
Who were the Indians? 24
The Indian wars 26
The road to Wounded Knee 28

5 LIFE IN THE AMERICAN WEST
The Mountain Men 30
Life on the range 32
On the trail 34
Frontier army 36
Frontier town 38
Pioneer life 40
Entertainment 42

6 LAW AND LAW-BREAKERS
Lawmen 44
Conmen 46
Badmen 48
Instant justice 50
Range wars 53

7 LEGACY OF THE 'OLD' WEST 55

Table of dates 56
New words 57
Further information 58
Index 59

1 THE STORY OF DANIEL BOONE

Young explorer

Above *The pioneer, Daniel Boone, 1734-1820.*

Opposite *In 1755 General Braddock's expedition against the French at Fort Duquesne was ambushed. Boone, who was driving a supply wagon, managed to escape from the slaughter.*

They were called the 'Long Hunters': a handful of rugged men who made long journeys westwards across the Appalachian Mountains. They risked their lives to explore Kentucky and beyond — the forests, the rivers and the plains. The most famous was Daniel Boone.

Boone's grandfather, a Devonshire Quaker, came to America in 1717. He settled in Pennsylvania, one of the English colonies that stretched down the eastern coastline of the massive and lonely continent. Daniel was born there in 1734. Sixteen years later, his family moved to the western frontier of North Carolina.

Most of Boone's fellow colonists looked east across the Atlantic Ocean to Britain, their 'mother country'. To the west lay a wilderness, full of dangers. But some Americans, including the young and adventurous Boone, were eager to head into the unknown.

Boone's chance came in 1755. In that year Britain was at war with France on the American continent, where both countries had colonies. Boone joined General Braddock's ill-fated expedition against Fort Duquesne (Pittsburgh) as a supply wagon driver. Their long march through wild and deserted country ended in disaster when the British troops were ambushed and cut to pieces by the French and their Indian allies. Boone managed to escape, but the expedition had fired him with an urge to explore the untamed land outside the frontiers of the colonies. Soon after the Braddock disaster, Boone married a 17-year-old girl named Rebecca. She was a true pioneer woman, who raised a fine family, and was often by his side when the going got rough.

Hunter and soldier

Below *In 1775 Boone and his fellow explorers built this fort, named Boonesborough, in the heart of Kentucky.*

In 1769 Boone reached Kentucky through the Cumberland Gap on a route the Indians called the Warrior's Path. Kentucky seemed a paradise, with vast herds of buffalo and a wealth of deer, turkey and other animals. Boone spent two years there as a trapper. Life was tough and dangerous, and the Indians were often hostile: he was captured once, and had all his furs and hides stolen on another occasion. He returned to North Carolina and immediately planned an expedition to settle in Kentucky. His family set out in 1773, but were forced to retreat after a fight with Indians in which his son James was killed.

Early in 1775, the year the American colonies rebelled against Britain, Boone headed for Kentucky again on

Indian trails that would become the famous Wilderness Road. He and his travelling companions built a fort named Boonesborough in Boone's honour, deep in Indian territory. When the American War of Independence broke out, Boonesborough was in danger because most Indians sided with the British, not the Americans who were always seizing their land.

In 1778 Boone, then a captive of the Shawnee Indians, heard that Boonesborough was to be attacked. He escaped, running 260km (160 miles) in four days, and entered the fort just in time. The siege of Boonesborough lasted ten desperate days, before the attacking Indians were beaten off. Ironically, Boone, the fort's saviour, was accused of collaborating with the Indians during his captivity. Fortunately the court-martial found him innocent, and he was promoted to major.

Below *A map of Boone's America. The dotted lines show the routes Boone took when exploring beyond the boundaries of the English colonies.*

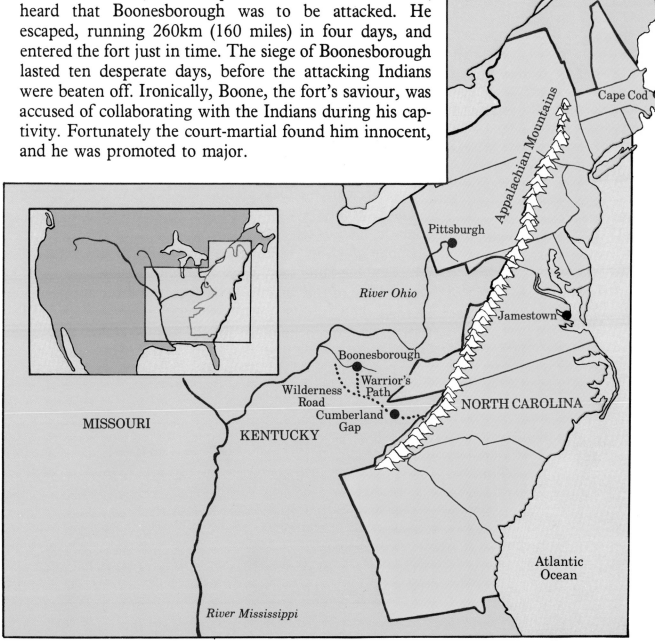

The legend

Above *This poster, printed in 1875, advertises homes and land for sale in the West.*

The War of Independence ended in 1783. Boone, now a colonel, thought that he was rich, but lawyers back east tried to prove that his lands were not legally his. Over the next few years, Boone argued constantly with lawyers about the legal right to his property. To the east he was a poor debtor, in the West a legend!

In 1799 Boone and Rebecca walked westwards to settle in Missouri, gazed at by thousands along the way. Missouri was then Spanish territory, and welcoming officials made him a magistrate. When Missouri became American, Boone's new land was grabbed by the US government because it was Spanish-registered. But they were shamed into returning part of it to Boone because of the great man's achievements. He paid off most of his debts in Kentucky, and returned to Missouri with fifty cents in his pocket!

Boone died in 1820, aged 86. Already a legend in America, his fame soon spread throughout the world. He was master of the wilderness, a great explorer and leader of men who, unlike most pioneers, liked and admired Indians, although he often fought against them. He was even adopted by Chief Blackfish of the Shawnee as his son. He symbolises the spirit that led so many thousands to head into the unknown West.

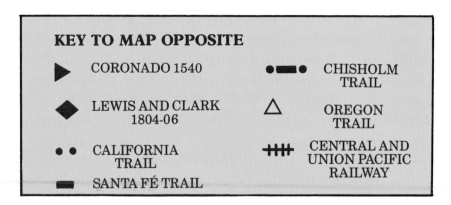

KEY TO MAP OPPOSITE

► CORONADO 1540	●■● CHISHOLM TRAIL
◆ LEWIS AND CLARK 1804-06	△ OREGON TRAIL
●● CALIFORNIA TRAIL	╫╫╫ CENTRAL AND UNION PACIFIC RAILWAY
▬ SANTA FÉ TRAIL	

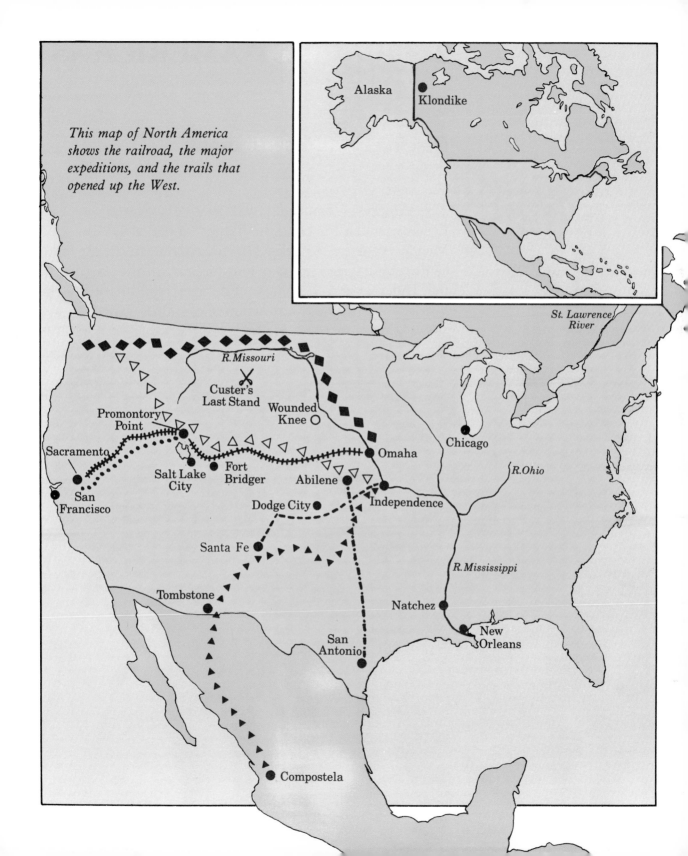

This map of North America shows the railroad, the major expeditions, and the trails that opened up the West.

Alaska

Klondike

St. Lawrence River

R. Missouri

Custer's Last Stand

Wounded Knee

Chicago

R. Ohio

Promontory Point

Sacramento

Salt Lake City

Fort Bridger

Abilene

Omaha

San Francisco

Dodge City

Independence

Santa Fe

R. Mississippi

Tombstone

Natchez

San Antonio

New Orleans

Compostela

2 THE FIRST AMERICANS

Discovery and settlement

The American continent was first 'discovered' by Leif Eriksson when his band of Vikings landed at L'Anse-aux-Meadows, on present-day Newfoundland, in the eleventh century. They did not stay long because of the hostility of the Indians and Eskimos. The next landmark in the history of America was when Columbus sailed to the 'New World' in 1492. He believed that he had discovered the Indies — India — which is why he called the natives 'Indians': in fact he had reached the West Indies.

White men first marched into the west of the American continent in 1540. They were Spaniards heading north

from Mexico, seeking the Seven Cities of Gold — which turned out to be Indian dwellings of mud and stone shining in the sun. Spanish influence in the West lasted until the nineteenth century, and many of today's American cities have Spanish names. Spaniards also explored in the east, but fewer settled there. The French were in the east soon after the Spaniards. They established settlements along the St. Lawrence River in Canada, and built bases in the south along the Mississippi River.

The first English colony was founded at Jamestown in Virginia in 1607 to promote trade. In 1620 the Pilgrim Fathers landed at Cape Cod in what is now Massachusetts, seeking religious freedom. Inevitably, France and England fought for mastery in America. Canada became British in 1760 when Montreal fell, a year after General Wolfe's great victory at Quebec. Now Britain was master of the Atlantic coastline and eastern Canada — but some of her colonists were beginning to think of themselves as Americans, not Britons.

Above *A portrait of Christopher Columbus, who sailed to the 'New World' in 1492.*

In 1540 Coronado led an expedition of Spaniards from Mexico which reached Kansas and Texas. But he failed to find the Seven Cities of Gold.

Above *Benjamin Franklin (left), a leading American public figure, helps to draft the Declaration of Independence in 1776.*

Above *George Washington, America's first President from 1789-96.*

From colony to superpower

Free from the French menace, some Americans openly began to resent being governed by a Parliament sitting 3,000 miles away in London. They were unhappy at being forced to pay taxes by a Parliament in which there were no Americans to represent their wishes. Successive British governments made things worse until rebellion broke out in 1775. It was a civil war in which Americans fought on both sides, and which Britain found hard to fight from so far away. The Americans had a great leader in George Washington, and when the French joined in against Britain — where the war was unpopular — it was only a matter of time before the British gave in. Independence, declared in 1776, was a fact by 1783.

There were still Spanish and French in the West, but there was no stopping the advance westwards by American pioneers. In the east, Americans and Britons were at war again in 1812. The Americans failed to take Canada, but by 1815 the British finally gave up the idea of interfering in America's future.

The next great crisis was the Civil War (1861-65) between the North (the Union) and the South (Confederates), mostly about states' rights, including the keeping of slaves. The South was defeated, the slaves were freed, and America remained united. But in the hour of victory, Abraham Lincoln, the President, and perhaps the greatest of all Americans, was assassinated.

Since the Civil War, the USA has gone from strength to strength. Millions of Europeans flocked there for a better life in the last century. It was a leading world power by 1900, and is now the richest and most powerful nation on earth. Today's Americans owe much to the pioneering spirit of their ancestors who carved a proud nation out of the wilderness of the West.

Above *Abraham Lincoln, President of the Union from 1861-65.*

Below *Lincoln's assassination: on 14 April 1865, Southerner John Wilkes Booth shot Lincoln as he was watching a play at Ford's Theatre in Washington.*

3 MOVING WESTWARDS

Land hunger

Below *At the siege of the Alamo in 1836, the legendary figures of Jim Bowie and Davy Crockett both died a hero's death at the hands of Mexican soldiers.*

It is impossible to exaggerate the importance of the westward movement in American history. Instead of looking eastwards to Europe, thousands, then millions, headed westwards until by the end of the nineteenth century there was no frontier left.

Why did men and women go west? They were curious to see what lay over the horizon, beyond the mountains, and then the broad sweep of the Mississippi River. But mostly it was the hunger for land that drove them on. A vital event which allowed westward expansion was the

purchase of Louisiana Territory by President Jefferson in 1803. For a mere $15 million he bought the entire area from the Mississippi Valley to the Rocky Mountains. An expedition under Meriwether Lewis and William Clark explored the area and beyond to the Pacific between 1804-06, opening American eyes to the West's possibilities. Soon thousands of settlers were on the move.

Meanwhile Spain's empire in the Americas had crumbled. Mexico became independent in 1821. American settlers flooded into Texas which was then Mexican territory. In the mid-1830s the Americans rebelled against their Mexican overlords. In 1836 they were defeated at the siege of the Alamo in which two legendary Americans — Jim Bowie and Davy Crockett — were killed.

In 1846 the USA went to war with Mexico. Mexico lost out badly: Texas became part of America in 1847 and, just a week after gold was found in California in 1848, the peace treaty gave it to the USA.

Covered wagons

The early pioneers travelled vast distances in covered wagons. Their destination was Oregon on the north-west coast. From the early 1840s, covered wagons rolled there from Independence and other small towns along the Missouri River. The distance was more than 3,000 km (1,850 miles), so they set out in spring when the pasture was good and the weather mild. Oregon had to be reached before the snows came.

Oregon was disputed territory between Britain and America. The pioneers, if they survived the ordeal of the journey, would make it American and be rewarded with land. The first great crossing from east to west was made in 1843 by 200 families in 120 wagons, averaging 15 km (9 miles) a day. Most rode in converted farm wagons that held basic possessions. The big 'prairie schooners' were mostly used on the south-western trade route to Santa Fé.

There was little trouble from Indians on the Oregon Trail in those early days. The main dangers were river crossings, precipitous mountain passes and killer diseases, especially cholera. If a wagon broke down it had to be left. Time was all important. The wagon ruts of these pioneers can be seen in many places in the West to this day.

Some broke off to follow the California Trail, which really came into its own when gold was found there in 1848. Meanwhile, the Mormons, a religious sect persecuted because they allowed a man to have more than one wife, headed for Utah, led by Brigham Young. Some walked pulling their possessions in handcarts. There they built Salt Lake City and 'made the desert bloom'.

Above *A portrait of Brigham Young, who led an expedition of Mormons to Utah where they founded Salt Lake City in 1847.*

Below *Crossing rivers was one of the many dangers facing pioneers on the Oregon Trail.*

Gold rush!

Gold! In the nineteenth century news of a big gold strike swept whole continents. Ships set sail from ports around the world, packed with prospectors, while others came by land. They were driven on by greed and the dream of fabulous wealth. Only a handful would find gold but gold fever inspired countless thousands.

The most famous gold strike was in California in 1848, when John Marshall found gold in a river near a sawmill on the property of his employer, John Sutter. Sutter tried to keep the find a secret, but failed. Soon news reached the tiny village of San Francisco, and spread beyond. A frantic gold rush started as thousands of prospectors headed for California — across America, the Pacific Ocean and the fever-ridden swamps of Panama. It was now 1849 and the famous 'forty-niners' were on their way.

Very few prospectors made fortunes. It was the traders and the men who had the money to organize mines who grew fabulously rich. Some owners became multi-millionaires while the state of California, and then the nation as a whole, became richer and richer. Silver, too, was found in some places in huge quantities.

In 1898, news spread that gold had been found in the Klondike in Canada near the Alaskan border, and the last great rush began. It was the most rugged of them all, for just getting there was a heroic ordeal. When most Klondike 'Stampeders' had finally made it, the best gold-bearing areas had already been staked out. And, as usual, machines soon took over the mining operation from men who until then had mostly panned for gold by hand. Fifty thrilling years had come to an end.

Below *Methods of finding gold: panning, and using a cradle.*

1

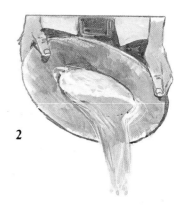

2

Cross-section of the hopper placed in the cradle

To find gold the hopper was placed on the apron and the cradle was rocked. Earth was put into the hopper and water was poured on top. The sediment containing the gold drained out through the holes in the base of the hopper and was caught in the riffles.

Perforated base

THE HOPPER

Apron

Riffles

Rockers

THE CRADLE

1. Water and earth believed to contain gold was swilled around in a flat pan.
2. The light muddy water was then poured off leaving the heavier gold in the pan.

19

Steamboats and stages

Steamboats were operating in some areas of the West before stagecoaches and railroads. In 1811, the *New Orleans* began trading between New Orleans and Natchez on the Mississippi, and soon steamboats were carrying cargoes of cotton and coal, as well as businessmen, gamblers and crooks. By the 1840s there were more than 2,000 steamboats on western rivers.

The success of the steamboats relied on the skill of the captains and pilots. Pilots had to know every snag on every river, while captains were often entrusted with entire stocks of cotton and sugar to sell down river for plantation owners at the best price. Farmers and ranchers trusted them too, sometimes unwisely.

Stagecoaches played a vital role in the opening up of the West. It was an uncomfortable and sometimes dangerous way to travel — Indians and outlaws could see to that — but stages covered many areas where there were no railroads or rivers. The most famous stagecoach firm was Wells Fargo, Henry Wells and William Fargo having built up a transportation empire in Gold Rush California, then elsewhere. Stage drivers were tough characters, one of the toughest being Charlie Parkhurst. After his death it was found that he was a she!

The most thrilling firm was the Pony Express linking California and Missouri. This was a fast mail service: eighty daring boy riders carried mail in a giant relay race backwards and forwards, changing horses regularly. They braved every hazard from appalling weather to hostile Indians. One team managed 3,000 km (1,850 miles) in six days. But in 1861, after eighteen months of world-wide fame, a transcontinental telegraph ended the adventure.

Below *Wells Fargo stagecoaches were always vulnerable to attack by bandits.*

Rails across the West

One of the greatest days in America's history was when the nation was spanned by rail. Building the railroad had been a rugged, often dangerous, adventure. It was undertaken by two companies. From Omaha, Nebraska, the Union Pacific workforce headed west, while the Central Pacific headed east from California.

Work on the 3,000 km (1,850 miles) project could not begin until the Civil War had ended in 1865. There were many war veterans in Union Pacific's workforce, along with Irish, Germans and other immigrants. They were often attacked by Indians who rightly saw the 'Iron Horse' as a threat to their freedom. Meanwhile, in the far

Below An historic moment in the opening up of the West: the Central Pacific and Union Pacific railroads meet at Promontory Point, Utah, on 10 May 1869.

west, white workers were hard to find because most were seeking gold. So Charley Crocker, Central Pacific's boss, hired Chinese workers. Many sneered, considering the Chinese no match for the task of cutting a way through the mountains, but the sneers died away. The Chinese proved able, strong and brave.

The two railroads met on 10 May 1869, at Promontory Point, Utah. When the news that the West was now linked by rail to the rest of the USA was flashed across the continent by telegraph, there were universal rejoicings.

The transcontinental railroad opened up the Plains to millions of easterners and foreigners, and made fortunes for bosses. Only the Indians suffered. Troops could now be rushed west, while the buffalo on which the Indians depended were slaughtered faster than ever, some even by hunters riding the 'Iron Horse'. As for the railroad builders, few of their names are known, but their achievements will never be forgotten.

Above *Shooting buffalo from trains was great sport in the West. Sportsmen enjoyed it but the Indians, who depended on the buffalo for food and clothes, suffered badly as a result.*

4 NATIVE AMERICANS

Who were the Indians?

Below *The earliest inhabitants of the American continent crossed over the Bering Strait from Asia to Alaska thousands of years ago.*

About 30,000 years ago the ancestors of today's native Americans started crossing from Asia to America via the Bering Strait to Alaska, the narrow strait being then almost a land bridge. Down the centuries, they headed south, some choosing places to settle, others crossing into Central and South America.

By the 1600s there were probably less than a million Indians in what is now the USA. They were divided into

tribes and led very different lives in the forests, on the plains and prairies, and in the mountains. Most Indians farmed, and nearly all fought slow-motion battles on foot before they discovered horses, the descendants of animals that had escaped from the Spanish, or ones they got from traders. Suddenly their whole lifestyle was changed, though women continued to do the hard work while men hunted and fought.

Fighting became thrilling with the coming of the horse. On the Plains it became an even greater feat to touch an enemy with a 'coup stick' than to kill him. War became an exciting game — until wars with the white man started. The white man took Indians' land and destroyed the buffalo which Indians used for food, shelter and clothing. With the coming of the white man, their world was doomed.

The Indian wars

Above *General George Custer (1839-76), commander of the Seventh Cavalry.*

Above *Sitting Bull, a chief of the Sioux. Born in 1834, he was killed on his reservation in 1890.*

The story of the Indian wars in America is a classic example of history repeating itself. White men came and were often welcomed by the Indians. Soon, tensions grew, usually over the white man's lust for land. Wars started which were nearly always won in the end by the better-armed, more numerous whites.

The wars started on the east coast of America in the seventeenth century. By the early 1800s, the Indians in the east had been killed or driven westwards. By the 1850s, it was the turn of the Indians of the West to come into conflict with the advancing, land-hungry Americans.

The Plains Indians, under great chiefs like Red Cloud, Sitting Bull and Crazy Horse, fought fiercely. Magnificent warriors on horseback, the Sioux, Cheyenne and Arapaho defeated General Custer and his Seventh Cavalry at the Battle of the Little Bighorn in 1876 — Custer's 'Last Stand'. But now, with the buffalo almost gone, and with trains bringing troops in fast, the army was able to crush tribe after tribe. The survivors were put on reservations which were usually on poor land that the whites did not want.

There were never enough Indians to defeat the Americans in the long run. Besides, so great was the Indian love of personal freedom that Indian leaders rarely had total control of their men in the way that even junior American officers had. Even with such control, the Indians could not have held out for long against overwhelming odds and far greater fire power. Yet their heroism will never be forgotten.

Opposite *The battle of the Little Bighorn in 1876: Custer's Seventh Cavalry were sent to fight a large force of Indians. Instead of waiting for support, Custer attacked. His unit of more than 250 soldiers was surrounded and all the men, including Custer, were wiped out. A single horse, Comanche, was the only survivor.*

The road to Wounded Knee

Above *An Apache leader, Geronimo (front row, third from the right) is pictured with his band of Indian warriors. They were taken from here to a prison camp in Florida at the end of the last Apache war in 1886.*

By the 1880s only the Apaches in the deserts and mountains of the south-west were still in action against the army. Under guerrilla leaders like Victorio and Geronimo they were almost impossible to find, let alone defeat. Mere handfuls of Apaches spread terror across Arizona and New Mexico, and across the Mexican border. Fortunately for the Americans, the Apaches were disunited and Apache scouts loyal to the Americans were able to track the 'hostiles' down. In 1886, the last fighting band was cornered and sent east for years of bitter exile.

With other Indians defeated and confined to reservations, peace seemed to have come to the West. But there was to be one last tragic battle. A Paiute named Wovoka foretold the disappearance of the whites. He did not preach war, but the despairing Sioux, miserable on their reservations in Dakota, misunderstood his message: some believed it spelt war.

War could have been avoided, but a weak Indian agent on a reservation, mistakenly fearing trouble, called for troops. The great Sitting Bull was wrongly suspected of master-minding the rebellion that never was and was shot by Indian police. Worse followed. The band of Chief Big Foot was rounded up by the Seventh Cavalry — Custer's old regiment — and misunderstandings led to the slaughter of men, women and children at a place called Wounded Knee. After it was over the victims were buried in mass, snow-covered graves. The Indian wars were over.

Below *The massacre at Wounded Knee: Chief Big Foot's body lies frozen in the snow after he and his band of Indians were slaughtered having been wrongly suspected of trying to start a rebellion.*

5 LIFE IN THE AMERICAN WEST

The Mountain Men

Above *Mountain Men gather for their annual spree at a rendezvous camp in the hills. They often spent all the money they had earned from hunting over the last year in just one week!*

Not long after the Lewis and Clark expedition from the Pacific to Missouri in 1806, other Americans headed west. They were probably the toughest white men ever seen in the West. They were called Mountain Men, but they roamed deserts and plains as well.

They hunted for beaver, whose fur was fashionable in the east and in Europe at the time: men wore beaver hats and women wore the fur as trimmings.

The Mountain Men blazed trails all over the West. They were mostly 'loners' who lived like Indians, fought with and against them, and often married Indian girls.

Some became famous, like Jim Bridger, Jebediah Smith, and Jim Beckwourth, a half negro who became a Crow Indian chief.

Every year these loners met at a rendezvous camp. They met there with traders who, in exchange for furs, supplied the Mountain Men with tools, weapons and other provisions. Between business, the Mountain Men had a riotous time horse-racing, playing cards, getting drunk, and sometimes spending all their money in one giant spree. Then it was back to work for another year.

When beaver fur went out of fashion in the 1830s, Mountain Men had to find new jobs. Few could settle down to farming and most became guides to wagon trains, army scouts, or just wanderers, watching the West they knew and loved become tame.

Above *Jim Bridger, one of the Mountain Men.*

Life on the range

The cowboy is the most legendary figure of the 'Wild West'. He seems romantic enough now — and there are still some cowboys in the West — but the real cowboy was far from a romantic figure.

The cowboy was a hired hand on horseback, a tough, underpaid working man. He preferred riding to walking, disliked settlers — calling them 'sodbusters' or 'nesters' — and loathed sheep and anyone who kept them. He refused to eat mutton and claimed that sheep ruined the grass on the range and fouled waterholes.

The cowboy got up around 4 a.m. In spring and autumn cattle were rounded up, new calves branded and cattle selected for market. When barbed wire was introduced in the 1870s it simplified life on the range, but there were still plenty of jobs to do: branding, breaking horses in, finding stray cattle, putting out prairie fires, and mending fences.

Until the 1880s, the cattle were Longhorns, descendants of Spanish cattle brought to the 'New World' in the sixteenth century. Their horns sometimes measured more than 2 metres (2.2 yards) from tip to tip. New breeds from Britain, especially Herefords, improved stock from the 1880s onwards. Longhorns are now kept as pets or 'stars' in Western films.

The clothes cowboys wore were based on what Mexican cowboys — vaqueros — used. They included the leather leg protectors called chapajeros. Texan cowboys also adapted the Mexican saddle, with its horn designed to help lasso cattle. Texas was the largest cattle state, though cattle ranching slowly spread all across the West.

Below *Cowboys occasionally took time off from the hard task of rounding up the cattle to relax on the range.*

On the trail

When the Civil War ended in 1865, Texas, having fought on the losing side, was in serious trouble. Her cattle industry had begun to boom before the war, but when the Texans returned from fighting, they found their ranches in ruins and their cattle scattered.

Fortunately, a northern cattle dealer called Joseph McCoy believed in the future. He built a cattle town called Abilene in Kansas. The new railroad ran through it and he sent messengers to Texas to tell cattlemen to drive their cattle to his 'cowtown'. From there the cows would be sent by rail to Chicago, which would soon be the nation's beef capital.

The Texas cattlemen answered his call, and the great cattle drives began. Tough trail bosses ran the drives like a military operation. In 1871, 600,000 Longhorns were driven northwards up the great Chisholm Trail, and other smaller trails. Trail herds took about four months to reach Abilene, and other cowtowns that soon sprang up.

There were many hazards on the trail. Cowboys were attacked by outlaws and Indians, and men and beasts drowned in rough river crossings. But the greatest hazard of all was a stampede, which could be started by a flash of lightning, a sudden sound, or even nothing at all! Somehow, the cowboys had to get the herd in a circle until the cattle calmed down. Stampedes could last for days and some cowboys were killed in them, and buried on the 'lone prairie'.

When the 'cowtown' was reached the cowboys were paid off. Not surprisingly, they went wild after their four-month ordeal on the trail.

Opposite *A stampede was the biggest threat to cowboys as they drove vast herds of cattle from Texas to cowtowns like Abilene. Sometimes cowboys were crushed to death under the hooves of hundreds of panicking cattle.*

Frontier army

Above *It was not often that soldiers in the small US frontier army were called into action. For the most part their lives followed a dull routine as they waited to be called upon to fight.*

The army in the West had a very difficult job. When the Civil War ended in 1865 most soldiers went home, and a mere 15,000 men — the equivalent of a small football crowd — were left to control the entire area west of the Mississippi.

Pay was poor, promotion slow, and before the Civil War only officers were allowed to have their wives with them. The troops were not the laughing heroes of many Western films, nor the monsters of some modern Westerns, but professionals doing their best in the face of conflicting orders. One moment they were fighting 'hostile' Indians who were only protecting their land; the next, trying to stop 'whites' from invading Indian reservations — for governments kept changing their minds about

the 'Indian problem'.

Boredom and loneliness were the soldiers' usual enemies, then suddenly there would be action that could end in torture and death. Between the action the men lived in their forts and small outposts built of stone or wood. Food could be good and varied in hunting areas, but usually the men had a steady diet of pork or beef, dried vegetables and 'hard tack' — hard biscuits.

There were cavalry and infantry in the West and a few artillery. They fought a few big battles and many skirmishes. There were 938 engagements between 1865-98 in which 56 officers and 860 men died. This army recruited many different nationalities: Americans, Irish, Britons, and also the 'Black' regiments. When repeating rifles were given to them in the mid-1860s they had a great advantage over their enemy. Yet fighting the Indians remained a difficult, dangerous and often deadly business.

Above *This photograph, taken in 1873, shows officers and their wives enjoying an afternoon's croquet at Fort Bridger in Wyoming.*

Frontier town

'Town' was an all-purpose word in the West. It could include a booming, gold rich city like San Francisco or a few shacks huddled together on the plains.

Towns of every sort sprang up in California during the gold rush. Most were all-male settlements at first, lonely miners having to dance with other miners, just as cowboys often had to do at dances on the ranch. Women were so rare in Gold Rush California that even the least beautiful could be sure of a husband, while in Oregon a saloon keeper charged money for the pleasure of looking at his wife. Plenty paid . . .

Cowtowns were wild places, but even they were no wilder than 'end-of-track' railroad towns. Weary railroad workers headed for tents and shacks in search of entertain-

Below *Not all Western towns were wild and lawless. This photograph, taken in 1887, shows a chemist's shop in a respectable community in Dodge City, Kansas.*

ment and 'rot-gut' whisky. Nicknames for such drinks included 'coffin varnish', 'snake poison', 'tarantula juice' and 'stagger soup'. Lawmen who could cope with 'end-of-track' towns could handle anything.

A few towns in pioneering areas were respectable from the start. Others became so when the railhead had moved on, while some ex-cowtowns banned all drinking once the cowboys had gone.

Churches and schools were features of every growing frontier community, while even a cowtown had its respectable quarter on 'the right side of the tracks' — the railroad tracks. Towns in the West were important centres for settlers and their families to shop, make friends and enjoy the entertainments. A visit to a town was often an exciting event in their lonely lives.

Above *Saloons in frontier towns were rough places where gambling and drinking often led to fights between rowdy railroad workers, cowboys, or gold prospectors.*

Pioneer life

Millions of Americans look back with pride on their grandparents and great-grandparents who endured hardships almost unimaginable today. These were the 'sodbusters', who proved that the Plains, once called the 'Great American Desert', could be tamed and made into good farming land.

The pioneers endured harsh and lonely lives. 'I fought bedbugs and flies all summer,' wrote one pioneer woman, who scrubbed plank floors and 'mingled my tears with the suds'. The loneliness could be intolerable in places where one's nearest neighbour could be a day's ride away. The first western pioneers headed for Oregon, but once it proved possible to plough up the Plains thousands moved

Below *In the West, women worked hard to build homes and farm the land to provide for their families.*

there, encouraged by the government's offer of cheap land. The new railroads increased the flood of settlers, many thousands coming from all parts of Europe.

The pioneers were the truest heroes and heroines in the winning of the West. They faced fewer Indian attacks than their parents and grandparents had back east, but when attacks came they could be terrible. It is true that the whites were responsible for nearly every Indian war, but that does not alter the nightmare that hit many pioneering families.

Gradually, small communities were built up, which became towns. Schools soon opened, some children having to travel a long way to get to them. Lucky pioneers lived near water, but in the 1880s simple windmills were used all over the Plains to pump water from wells. Fortunately, there was nearly always a strong wind on the Plains to power them!

Above *A pioneering family stand outside their house which is made from blocks of earth.*

41

Entertainment

Above *Western townspeople longed for entertainment. Drama companies toured the country and played to packed audiences.*

Western townspeople and lonely settlers longed for entertainment. Even before the railroads came, entertainers travelled all round the frontier areas. Gold Rush California was a magnet for them, and once the railroads were built, showbusiness boomed.

Leading comedians, top actors and singers all toured the West. Whole opera companies on special trains sang their way across the continent. In San Francisco Italian fishermen, who knew the popular operas by heart, were brought in to swell the chorus!

Showboats, which were whole boats given over to entertainment, appeared on western rivers, while Western shows were popular in the east and west alike. The finest was *Buffalo Bill's Wild West*, run by and starring 'Buffalo Bill' Cody, so called because he had once been a mighty

buffalo hunter. One of the few westerners who genuinely liked Indians, he employed many straight off the warpath: they believed that it was better to perform in his show than to rot on a reservation.

'Buffalo Bill' toured America, Britain and Europe, his most famous trip being to Britain in 1887, the year of Queen Victoria's Golden Jubilee. The queen and hundreds of thousands of Britons loved the show, especially one of its stars, Annie Oakley — 'Little Sure Shot' — who could shoot as well as any man in the world.

Way out west, the poet and writer, Oscar Wilde, turned up at the tough mining town of Leadville, Colorado, and lectured on *The Ethics of Art*. The miners must have been stunned, but they elected Wilde 'the Prince of good fellows' because he could drink more than any of them!

Above *Annie Oakley, an expert shot and a star of 'Buffalo Bill's Wild West' show.*

6 LAW AND LAW-BREAKERS

Lawmen

Above *James Butler 'Wild Bill' Hickok, a famous gunfighter who was marshal of Abilene in 1871. Born in 1837, he was shot dead while playing cards in 1876.*

The term 'Wild West' is usually applied to the area west of the Mississippi and what happened there after the Civil War ended in 1865. Yet it was often even wilder before that. In such vast areas, official lawmen were rarely seen, and sheriffs had a tough time trying to keep law and order.

After the war, men tried hard to establish law in the West, notably in the booming and violent cowtowns. After several wild seasons, the town of Abilene showed what could be done. In 1869, Marshal Tom Smith tamed the wild Texans, forcing them to hand over their pistols until they left town. He used his sledgehammer fists to keep order.

Smith was later murdered, and James Butler 'Wild Bill' Hickok continued the good work. He used pistols, not fists, but seldom fired them: his reputation alone tamed most badmen. Another busy area for lawmen was Indian Territory, now Oklahoma, which was infested with outlaws. Many of them were strung up by that stern lawman, Judge Parker, after they had received the death sentence in court. There were also groups of lawmen, the most famous being the Texas Rangers. Another group was Pinkerton's detective agency.

Local sheriffs could raise posses to track down badmen, citizens riding with the lawmen. Gradually marshals, sheriffs, their deputies and ordinary frontiersmen built up a respect for law and order. By 1902, when Butch Cassidy and the Sundance Kid headed for South America, the wild days were almost over although even today, America has a problem fighting violent crime.

Below *'Wild Bill' Hickok killed Dave Tutt in a street duel in Springfield, Missouri, in 1865.*

Conmen

Above *The West was full of patent medicine men pretending they had a cure for every disease. Often their 'medicine' was little more than coloured water.*

The West was a paradise for conmen of every sort. Towns were full of crooked gamblers. Small pocket pistols, knives, weighted dice and all sorts of devices for cheating at cards were used to part 'suckers' from their money. One man, who ran a saloon, used to rob his clients after first drugging them. As for some gambling saloons in Gold Rush San Francisco, it was hard work escaping from them alive.

Patent medicine men descended like locusts on the West, claiming they could cure anything. Gallons of Hamlin's 'Wizard Oil', 'Blood Pills' and 'Cough Balsam' were sent from Chicago to the West each year, accompanied by a male vocal quartet singing its praises. One 'painless' dentist hired a band to drown out his victims' screams; another who pulled the wrong tooth out of gunfighter Clay Allison, was seized by his angry patient, who proceeded to extract the dentist's teeth until he was rescued by a crowd who heard his yells.

King of the conmen was 'Soapy' Smith, who got his name in Colorado when he convinced miners that the $5 sticks of soap he sold might have dollars under their wrappers. The first one he sold contained a $100 note, visible to the crowd while he wrapped it. The rush for the rest was tremendous, though nearly all contained just soap. In the Klondike Stampede he had the border town of Skagway 'sewn up' by his gang. There was even a phoney telegraph office for messages home. Many miners lost everything. Finally the town rose up against the gang. Soapy was killed and gang broke up.

Below *Conman 'Soapy' Smith (bearded) stands at the bar in Skagway, Alaska. He was killed by the townspeople in 1898.*

Badmen

Some Western badmen like Billy the Kid and Jesse James are famous to this day. Others deserve to be better known.

Such a one was Henry Plummer, who ran a large gang in the Montana goldfields, his spies marking coaches ripe for robbing. It helped that this honest-looking man got himself elected local sheriff, but finally he was caught and strung up by vigilantes.

Most Western gunfighters were mixtures of good and bad. Jesse and Frank James, and their cousins, the Youngers, were vicious products of the Civil War in Kansas and Missouri. They were southerners, and as the

Below *The 'Wild Bunch': front row, from left to right, Harry Longabaugh (the Sundance Kid), Ben Kilpatrick, Butch Cassidy; back row, Bill Carver and Harvey Logan (Kid Curry).*

South lost, many regarded them and their gangs of bank and train robbers as heroes, not villains. Finally, the authorities hired Bob Ford, an ex-member of the James gang, to kill Jesse.

Solo killers included John Wesley Hardin, a Texan who boasted of killing 44 men. He shot one man through a hotel wall for snoring, and was finally shot from behind in a bar in 1894.

Often there were battles between gangs of badmen. The most famous gunfight was at the O.K. Corral in Tombstone, Arizona in 1881. It featured the Earp brothers and 'Doc' Holliday, none of whose records was spotless, defeating the Clantons in a fight that took less than a minute (It takes longer in films!). Wyatt Earp himself lived to be 80.

Above *Banks were easy targets for gangs of robbers, led by men like Jesse James, and Butch Cassidy and the Sundance Kid.*

Instant justice

The sheer size of the West and the lack of lawmen made instant justice almost inevitable. 'Instant' usually meant that the victims — often innocent — were hanged without trial. This process was also called 'a necktie party' or being 'jerked to Jesus'!

Sometimes the men who carried out this instant justice, often called vigilantes, had right on their side. By 1850, Gold Rush San Francisco was swarming with criminals, the worst being the 'Sydney Ducks', British ex-convicts from Australia. 200 citizens started a vigilance committee. They turned out when a bell rang, hanged a number of criminals, and disbanded themselves, having 'cleaned up' the town. It was not true justice, but it worked.

Alas, vigilantes too often got rid of enemies so they could grab their land or property. They often got away with it because the army could not intervene unless ordered to by the government.

Some instant justice was racial, as Mexicans and Indians found in California. Some were hanged without being able to say a word in English in their defence. Some frontier judges were inefficient and corrupt. The notorious Judge Roy Bean had this to say when an Irishman had killed a Chinaman. 'Gents, this here court finds that the law is explicit on the killin' of a fellow man, but there ain't nothin' about knockin' off a heathen Chinee. Case dismissed! And the drinks is on Paddy there!'

Below *Groups of vigilantes often took the law into their own hands and hung criminals before giving them a chance to defend themselves in the law courts.*

Range wars

Waterholes, barbed wire, confrontations between big and small ranchers and between cattlemen and sheepmen could all cause range wars. The most famous was the Lincoln County War in New Mexico. The country was 'run' by two ruthless businessmen named Dolan and Murphy. They had the local sheriff in their pocket and the support of corrupt politicians in New Mexico's capital, Santa Fe. Small ranchers and farmers were forced to sell out to the 'House', as Dolan and Murphy's store was called, or else . . .

Against them were two newcomers, Englishman John Tunstall and Canadian lawyer, Alexander McSween. In 1878, Tunstall, a businessman rancher, was murdered by some 'House' killers. One of his cowboys, Billy the Kid, swore to avenge him. 'War' broke out, the climax being the five-day 'battle' of Lincoln, in which McSween was killed. Billy managed to escape and, despite legends to the contrary, turned bad for the first time in his life. Caught by an old friend turned lawman, Pat Garrett, he daringly escaped from jail just before he was due to hang, but Garrett finally shot him on 14 July 1881.

The other great range war was the Johnson County War in Wyoming in 1892. Local 'Cattle Kings' decided to wipe out the small men, claiming they were all rustlers. They hired 52 Texan gunfighters and invaded the county. They started badly when a cowboy named Nate Champion held them off in his cabin for a whole day before he was burnt out and killed. The invaders asked for cavalry help, having lied about the situation. They claimed to have won the war, but in fact they lost it. The small ranchers and settlers survived and peace came to the range.

Opposite In the Johnson County War in 1892, a cowboy named Nate Champion held up a gang of 50 Texan gunfighters for a whole day. Eventually he was burnt out of his hiding-place and shot dead.

Above *'Billy the Kid', one of the most famous gunfighters of the West. He was already a legend by the age of 21, when he was finally shot dead by Pat Garrett, the sheriff of Lincoln County.*

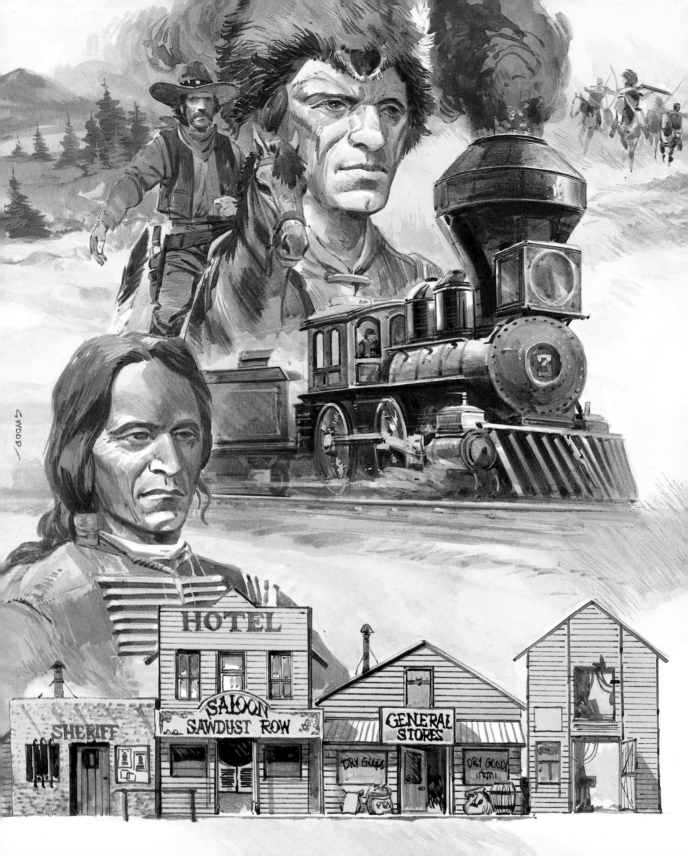

7 LEGACY OF THE 'OLD' WEST

As the years go by, the days of the 'Wild West' recede further and further into America's past. So what do they mean to America and to the world? Millions of Americans and thousands of Britons visit the West each year, and only those without imagination can fail to grasp something of what it took to tame it. Despite the colossal mineral wealth, the rich farmlands and the excellent cattle country of today's West, in those early days it took sheer hard work and guts to survive, let alone succeed.

Today's Americans are worlds away from those rough days. The frontier is now space, and the world is America's concern. Yet the 'Wild West' and its people are part of the nation's heritage. If the first pioneers — men like Daniel Boone — had not pushed westwards, or if Spain, France and Britain had not given way to the surging tide of pioneers, how different the world would be!

But what of today? Like all nations, the USA has its problems. Some see the violence in big cities, the number of firearms in use and the plight of the Indians as a throwback to the 'Wild West'. Yet why should the Old West be blamed?

Nothing can alter the fact that the epic of the West is a key part of American history. It is an epic of people who helped make a great nation out of land that they explored, tamed, sometimes cruelly, and made mighty.

Opposite *The illustration shows a typical row of shops in a frontier town; an Indian warrior; a cowboy on horseback; a portrait of Daniel Boone; Custer's Last Stand; a pioneer woman and her child; and a railway engine.*

Table of dates

c **30,000 B.C.** First 'Indians' cross from Asia to Alaska.

1540 Coronado's expedition in search of the Seven Cities of Gold: the first white men in the West.

1607 First successful English colony founded at Jamestown, Virginia.

1734 Daniel Boone born.

1760 France loses Canada to Britain.

1775 American War of Independence begins. Boonesborough built in Kentucky.

1783 War of Independence ends, triggering off westward expansion.

1803 Louisiana Purchase from France.

1804-06 Lewis and Clark's expedition to the Pacific and back.

c **1810-40** The Mountain Men era.

1811 Steamboat Age on western rivers begins.

1820 Daniel Boone dies.

1821 First Americans arrive in Texas.

1836 Siege and fall of the Alamo. At San Jacinto, Texans win independence.

1843 First great wagon train to Oregon.

1846-48 War between the USA and Mexico.

1847 Brigham Young leads Mormons to Utah: founds Salt Lake City.

1848 Gold found in California.

1849 The 'Forty-Niners' head for California.

1856 Wars between Plains Indians and Americans begin.

1860-61 The Pony Express.

1861-65 American Civil War.

1865 Work begins on transcontinental railroad.

1867 Joseph McCoy builds first cowtown at Abilene, Kansas. First Texan cattle come to it up Chisholm Trail.

1869 America spanned by rail.

1871 'Wild Bill' Hickok becomes marshal of Abilene.

1874 Barbed wire first used in the West.

1876 Battle of the Little Bighorn — Custer's Last Stand. 'Wild Bill' Hickok murdered in Deadwood.

1878 Lincoln County War in New Mexico.

1881 Death of Billy the Kid. Gunfight at the OK Corral in Tombstone, Arizona.

1886 Last Apache outbreak led by Geronimo. End of 25 years of Apache wars.

1890 Death of Sitting Bull. Massacre at Wounded Knee ends Indian wars.

1892 Johnson County War in Wyoming.

1898 The Klondike Stampede. Last great gold rush.

1902 Butch Cassidy and the Sundance Kid leave West for South America.

New words

Assassinate To murder an important political figure.

Collaborate Working with someone else, often to help an enemy.

Colony A group of people who settle together in another country.

Conmen People who try to trick you into parting with your money.

Court Martial A court held by military men to try soldiers who have broken military law.

Debtor A person who owes money to another.

Exile A person who has been forced to stay away from his homeland.

Gambler Someone who tries to win money by betting on cards and other games.

Gold panning The process of trying to separate particles of gold dust from the sediment found in rivers, using a pan.

Gold strike The discovery of gold.

Hide The skin of an animal.

Immigrant A person who comes into a country to settle.

Magistrate A person who has the power to enforce laws.

Patent An official document giving one person the sole rights to make or sell a new invention, in this case medicine.

Pioneer A person who explores a country, preparing the way for others to follow.

Posse A body of men, authorised to enforce law and order, who ride out with the sheriff to track down criminals.

Prairie A vast, grassy plain with few trees.

Prairie Schooner A large covered wagon that transported families across the prairie. They were so big they looked like schooners (large sailing ships).

Prospectors People who mined for gold and silver.

Quakers A religious sect founded by George Fox c1650.

Rendezvous A meeting place.

Rustler A cattle or horse thief.

Skirmish A fight between small groups of soldiers.

'Sodbusters' The pioneers who created good farming land from barren soil.

Stampede A sudden wild running away of a large number of frightened cattle.

Telegraph An apparatus for sending messages to a distant place by means of wires and electricity.

Trapper A person who hunts for wild animals, using 'traps' to catch them.

Tributary A stream or river that flows into another larger one.

Vigilantes Groups of people in frontier areas who took the law into their own hands.

Further information

Places to visit

Museums The American Museum at Claverton near Bath has plenty on display about the West, while those interested in firearms will find every type of gun used in the West at the Tower of London.

There are Indian collections at London's Museum of Mankind, and in many of Britain's University Museums. Local libraries should be checked for details. Those interested in Western animals can find them in most wildlife parks. At Camphill in County Tyrone, Ulster, is an Ulster-American Folk Park, Ulster having close historical links with the USA.

Those with a serious interest in the West can join the English Westerners' Society. The secretary is at 29 The Tinings, Monkton Park, Chippenham, Wiltshire.

In America there are great museums like the Smithsonian Institution in Washington D.C. and the Museum of Natural History in New York. Every state has its historical society complete with museum, and there are hundreds of other museums and art galleries worth a visit.

Famous sites In America there are many monuments and sites that recall the history of the West. The Alamo in San Antonio is a good example. There are many areas in the West itself which have changed little since the pioneers crossed the Plains, especially in the National Parks. There are rodeos to be enjoyed where today's cowboys are put through their paces, and many places have large Indian populations.

Books

Brandon, William, *The American Heritage Book of Indians* (American Heritage 1961)

Elliot, Lawrence, *Daniel Boone, the Long Hunter* (Allen and Unwin 1977)

Gillett, James, *Six Years with the Texas Rangers* (Yale University Press 1963)

Jackson, Donald Dale, *Gold Dust* (Allen and Unwin 1981)

May, Robin, *The American West* (Macmillan 1982); *Indians* (Bison Books 1983); *Warriors of the West* (Look-In Books 1978); *The Wild West* (Macdonald 1978)

Newark, Peter, *Cowboys* (Bison Books 1982) Reliable fiction includes Elliott Arnold's *Blood Brother;* A. B. Guthrie's *The Way West;* and the novels of Jack Shaefer, including *Shane.* The Time-Life *Old West* series has thousands of photographs of the American West and its inhabitants.

Films

Most Westerns make the story of the West too romantic. The following dozen — which will appear occasionally on TV — are very good and reasonably accurate.

Red River (1948); *She Wore a Yellow Ribbon* (1949); *High Noon* (1952); *Shane* (1953); *Apache* (1954); *The Searchers* (1956); *Will Penny* (1967); *Butch Cassidy and the Sundance Kid* (1969); *Paint Your Wagon* (1969); *A Man Called Horse* (1970); *Jeremiah Johnson* (1972); *Ulzana's Raid* (1972).

Index

Abilene, Kansas 9, 34, 44, 56
Alaska 9, 19, 24, 47, 56
Alamo, battle of 14, 15, 56
Apache Indians 28, 56
Appalachian Mountains 4, 7
Arapaho Indians 26
Arizona 28, 49
Atlantic Ocean 4, 7, 11

Bean, Judge Roy 50, 51
Beckwourth, Jim 31
Beaver furs 30, 31
Billy the Kid 48, 53, 56
Boone, Daniel
  early life 4
  hunter and soldier 6, 7
  legend 8, 9, 55
Boonesborough 7, 56
Bowie, Jim 31, 32
Braddock, General 4
Bridger, Jim 31, 32
Britain 6, 7, 11, 12, 13, 16, 43, 56
Buffalo 6, 23, 25, 26, 43
'Buffalo Bill' Cody 42, 43

California 8, 15, 17, 18, 19, 21, 22, 38, 42, 51, 56
California Trail 8, 9, 17
Canada 11, 13, 19, 56
Cape Cod 7, 11
Cassidy, Butch 45, 48, 49, 56
Cattle 32, 33, 34, 53
Cheyenne Indians 26
Chicago 9, 34, 47
Chinese railway workers 23, 51
Chisholm Trail 8, 9, 34, 56
Civil War, the American 13, 22, 34, 36, 44, 48, 56
Clanton family 49
Clark, William 8, 15, 30, 56
Colorado 43, 47
Columbus, Christopher 10, 11

Conmen 46, 47
Coronado, Francisco 8, 11, 56
Cotton 20, 21
Cowboys 32, 33, 34, 38, 39
Crockett, Davy 14, 15
Cumberland Gap 6, 7
Custer, General 9, 26, 29, 55, 56

Dakota 29
Dodge City, Kansas 38

Earp, Wyatt 49
Entertainment 42, 43
Eriksson, Leif 10

Florida 28
Fort Bridger 9, 37
Fort Duquesne (see Pittsburgh)
'Forty-niners' 19, 56
France 4, 11, 12, 56
Franklin, Benjamin 12

Gambling 20, 31, 39, 46, 57
Garrett, Pat 53
Geronimo 28, 56
Gold 15, 17, 18, 19, 23, 38, 39, 48, 56, 57

Hardin, John Wesley 49
Hickok, 'Wild Bill' 44, 45, 56
Holliday, 'Doc' 49

Independence
  American War of, 6, 7, 8, 12, 56
  Declaration of 12
Independence, Missouri 16

James, Jesse 48, 49
Jamestown, Virginia 7, 11, 56
Jefferson, President 14
Johnson County War 53, 56

Kansas 11, 34, 38, 48, 56
Kentucky 4, 6, 7, 8, 56
Klondike, Yukon 9, 19, 47, 56

Lewis, Meriwether 8, 15, 30, 56
Lincoln, Abraham 13
Lincoln County War 53, 56
Little Bighorn, battle of 26, 56
Louisiana Purchase 14, 56

Maps
  of eastern America 7
  opening-up of the West 9
Massachusetts 11
McCoy, Joseph 34, 56
'Medecine' men 46, 47
Mexico 11, 14, 15, 28, 33, 51, 56
Mississippi River 7, 9, 11, 14, 15, 36, 44
Missouri 7, 8, 21, 30, 45, 48
Missouri River 9, 16, 20
Montana 48
Mormons 17, 56
Mountain Men 30, 31, 32, 56

Natchez, Mississippi 9, 20
Nebraska 22
New Mexico 28, 53, 56
New Orleans, Mississippi 20
North Carolina 4, 6, 7

Oakley, Annie 43
Oklahoma 45
Ohio River 7, 9
Omaha 22
Oregon 16, 17, 38, 40, 56
Oregon Trail 8, 9

Pacific Ocean 15, 18, 30, 56
Pennsylvania 4
Pinkerton's Detective Agency 45

Pittsburgh 4, 7
Pony Express 21, 56
Posses 45, 57

Sacramento, California 9
St Lawrence River, 9, 11
Saloons 38, 39, 46
Salt Lake City, Utah 9, 17, 56
San Antonio, Texas 9
San Francisco, California 9,
    18, 38, 42, 46, 50
Santa Fé, New Mexico 9, 16,
    53
Santa Fé Trail 8, 9
Shawnee Indians 7, 8
Sheriffs 44, 45, 48, 53
Showboats 42
Silver 19
Sioux Indians 26, 29
Sitting Bull 26, 29

Skagway, Alaska 47
Slavery 13
Smith, Jebediah 31
Smith, Marshal Tom 44
'Soapy' Smith 47
Spain 8, 10, 11, 12, 15
Springfield, Missouri 45
Stagecoaches 20, 21
Stampede 34, 57
Steamboats 20, 56
Sundance Kid 45, 46, 48, 49

Telegraph 21, 23, 47, 57
Texas 11, 15, 33, 34, 44, 50,
    53, 56
Texas Rangers 45
Tombstone, Arizona 4, 9, 56
Towns 38, 39, 41, 44, 45
    'cowtowns' 34, 38, 39, 44
    'end-of-track' 38

Utah 17, 22, 23, 56

Vigilantes 48, 50, 51, 57
Vikings 10
Virginia 11, 56

Wagons 16, 17
Warrior's Path 6, 7
Washington, George 12
Wells Fargo Company 21
'Wild Bunch', the 48
Wilderness Road 7
Wolfe, General 11
Wounded Knee, massacre of
    9, 28, 29, 56
Wyoming 37, 53, 56

Young, Brigham 17, 56
Younger family 48

Picture acknowledgements

The illustrations in this book were supplied by: BBC Hulton Picture Library 44; Denver Public Library Western Collection 20, 47; Kansas State Historical Society 8, 31, 38; Mansell Collection 4, 7; National Archives 26 (above), 28, 37, 50; Robin May Collection 22, 26 (below), 41, 43, 48, 53; Wells Fargo Bank History Room 18; Wyoming State Archives and Historical Department 33. The remainder are from the Wayland Picture Library.